A Self-Directed Journey

The Recipe

BY
SANDRA HARDING
AND
DINI PETTY

Published in 1999 by Self-Directed Learning Inc.

You may reach us at:

The Self-Directed Learning Place,
121 Old Forest Hill Road, Unit 1
Toronto, Ontario M5N 2N6
Fax (416) 256-0531
Phone 1 800 303-5013

Canadian Cataloguing in Publication Data

Harding, Sandra, 1939-
Petty, Dini, 1946-
A SELF-DIRECTED JOURNEY - THE RECIPE

ISBN 0-9684217-0-9

The information contained in this book
is for educational purposes only.
Self-Directed Learning is an educational process.
Any mental, physical or emotional changes
is the result of ones' ability to perceive and
direct their world as an individual.

Cover photograph: Korby Banner

Printed and assembled in Canada.

Table of Contents

*S*CATTER YOUR DREAMS ACROSS THESE PAGES,
LAY YOUR FEARS TO REST BETWEEN THESE LINES.
LET HOPES BE BORN HERE,
AMBITIONS RISE FROM YOUR THOUGHTS.
SOW THE SEEDS OF YOUR FUTURE HERE
AND LET IMAGES OF
GOOD, BAD, BEAUTIFUL, AND UGLY
FALL FROM YOUR MIND AND SOUL
ONTO THESE PAGES.
THEN TAKE WHAT YOU WANT
AND GO FORWARD INTO YOUR FUTURE.

-- DINI PETTY

THE BUTTERFLY LAYING EGGS

Dedication

I dedicate this book to all those who
use the recipe to walk the Self-Directed path with me.

-- SANDRA HARDING

———◖◗———

I dedicate this book to those who wish to
connect with instinct and learn to use it.
This way, you can break the old patterns and heal,
which builds a great life.

-- DINI PETTY

Acknowledgments

I would like to express my appreciation and love
to my husband Michael, my daughter Gail,
her husband David, and to my grandchildren
Matthew, Rhiannon and Gillian
for being my mirrors.

My heartfelt appreciation to my dear friend Dini,
for being Dini.

To Brian Bailey, who I love like a day in the kitchen.

My project manager, giftwrapper and songbird,
Kathy Padulo -- *Molte Grazie!*

Billy Newton-Davis from whom I learned
that anything is possible.

Sandra DiValentin for the beautiful artwork.

To David Chilton our Self-Publishing angel
for sharing his expertise.

All those who helped with the manuscript
and the manufacturing of the book.

Finally, to everyone from whom I received examples
of how Self-Directed Learning has helped
make their lives better.

-- Sandra Harding

Introduction

Self-Directed Learning provides understanding into how we can build our health, vitality, and prosperity. By using instinct we learn to become our own authority in making choices that best meet our needs.

I first developed my Self-authority to deal with a weight problem. I had to learn from my Self good eating habits. I did this during my 10 year relationship with Weight Watchers when I lost over 100 pounds in 1971 and kept it off. It took two years to shed the weight and I lectured for the other eight. I discovered that when I was fat I was undernourished.

In 1980, I opened a weight loss centre in Toronto. The programs incorporated nutrition, physical fitness, behavioral modification, and group discussions.

At the same time I began to study acupuncture, kinesiology, physiology, and the unconscious mind. I experienced that obesity was a symptom of Self-hatred. I never met a fat person, me included, who loved their body.

In 1982 I began to investigate the relationship between the language of low Self-esteem and muscle control. I soon changed the format used at the Centre from instructing people, to a method that enabled me to get information from each individual, with them as their own authority. I discovered I could do this by using kinesiology, as muscles were a direct communication link to instinct. This made sense to me as I always believed that body language and posture were indicators of Self-esteem.

Thus the concept of Self-Directed Learning was born. A program of goal setting and body balancing through the use of language and kinesiology.

I introduced the "basics" as a concept to ensure that people had enough to eat and had proper rest to counter, in my opinion, the propaganda about dieting that caused people to get fat and deplete their energy.

The Self-Directed weight loss program worked very well and people were losing weight and keeping it off. The thing I found amazing was they were doing this with minimum dietary restriction.

I focused on showing them how to eat what they intuitively and instinctively wanted; to trust their cravings, use common sense, and love their own hearts.

As they realized that they intuitively knew what to eat, they trusted their instinct and their Self-confidence grew. Finally they could direct their own eating. As they continued to succeed they naturally developed a language of high Self-esteem. This resulted in going with their instinct more and more in other areas of life and achieving their goals.

My first grandson Matthew was born in July of 1983. When he was seven months old he was diagnosed as having Twentieth Century disease, which meant he reacted to the environment, especially to foods. The intensity of the reactions were severe and medicine's interpretation of this disease and lack of solutions for it were overwhelming and unacceptable. At this point we decided to pursue other alternatives. I decided to employ the same Self-Directed technology that I was using at the Center for weight loss with Matthew. I began using muscle testing to communicate with his instinct which foods he could tolerate. We fed him those foods which tested positively to give him energy and he started improving. It was then I realized that it was the inside relationship between

Matthew's mind and body that determined whether he built up immunity or reacted to his environment. I called this concept Processing In/Out.

Processing In/Out meant communicating with the intelligence of instinct for Self-preservation and making this the authority. Over time I refined this to the relationship between instinct and intellect. I discovered that our instinct naturally processes information In/Out, putting our point of view and needs first. We learn, in our culture, to intellectually process language Out/In, putting other things before our own health needs. We call this perceptual dyslexia. We react to our Self and our environment as instinct and intellect process information with opposite values, creating internal conflict, which manifests in declined health.

We worked to re-educate intellect to Process In/Out, which aligned with instinct, and after two years Matthew had no symptoms. He had developed a sense for what foods he could eat. Imagine a Bubby believing her grandchild knew more about what he needed nourishment-wise then she did. What a revelation!

All this experience confirmed to me that instinct is the boss and intellect is the worker. Instinct receives its direction from Self. Self contains the map of our hearts desire. Tapping into and going with instinct builds energy, immunity, harmony, and prosperity. On the other hand, going against instinct contributes to disease, struggle, conflict, and expends a lot of energy.

I combined the best of what I learned and incorporated this understanding and technology into the programs at the Centre. For a while I called my work soul-directing skills. Over time, this became Self-Directing skills.

Our allergy program expanded out of the experience with Matthew. Word got around and soon other people with allergies were being referred to us. Over the years we have seen many people stop reacting by learning to Process In/Out, thus improving their health.

I first met Dini in May of 1995 after someone mentioned my work to her. When I heard Dini say she was coming to see me I was ready to meet a soul sister.

In 14 years of coaching Self-Direction I had yet to meet a student who I heard so able to express her Self with so much integrity. To me, Dini is one of Canada's treasures, best interviewers, and number one talk show hosts.

I saw a tormented soul with low Self-esteem who had given up on her dreams. She was tied in a knot in her private life. After getting to know her, I saw a Self-confident, articulate, and very beautiful woman in her public life.

After beginning her Self-Directed Journey, I was impressed by how quickly Dini connected with her Self.

When I expressed the importance of food, water, and rest as the basic needs we have to fulfill in order to hear instinct, Dini committed to incorporating these fundamental components into her daily life. Then I introduced the concept of her instinct leading with her intellect following. Dini quickly related this idea to the times in her life when she followed her instinct and how it always steered her correctly. By fulfilling the basics and letting her instinct lead, I watched Dini transform the direction of her life.

I heard Dini begin to value her Self and as she did I watched her make her dreams a reality. Her confidence grew with each goal she achieved. Low Self-esteem was transformed into high Self-esteem and her health improved. I saw her discover her sense of purpose, watched her relationships improve, and witnessed the ratings for her TV show jump. As a result, I wanted to have Dini speak to people about Self-Directed Learning and asked her to help me get my message out. She agreed and we became partners.

What I want is to present my recipe to develop an automatic reflex, to do the basics and to get in touch with instinct. I want to help people learn to use instinct and intellect so that they can Self-Direct to build Self-confidence and Self-esteem. Imagine experiencing the good feeling and tremendous energy boost that comes from being true to Self and having a positive influence on those around you.

What I discovered I have put into this book to send you off on your own Self-Directed Journey.

Symbols and language are very important to me in my quest to understand my Self. Because of this, I have used the four stages in the birth of a butterfly to symbolize the transformation that occurs during the Self-Directed Journey. Throughout the book, I refer to 'Self' as singular. I believe we are all individual parts of one collective Self. This is where we connect with each other.

Dini's personal story will give you an idea of how she made her transformation from struggle to prosperity. By using my recipe, she greatly improved all aspects of her life.

The poem 'New Beginning', which is on the next page, represents the moment Dini recognized that her transformation was occurring. I think from reading it you will get an idea of things to come.

Bon Voyage

Sandra Harding

New Beginning

WHEN MY LIGHT IS DIMMING
I WILL LOOK BACK TO THIS POINT
AND KNOW THAT FROM HERE ON
I LIVED FOR ME.

I DID WHAT I WANTED TO DO
I SPOKE FROM MY HEART
AND SPOKE ONLY THE TRUTH TO MY SELF.

I PUT MY SELF FIRST
I BELIEVED IN ME AND MY TALENT
IN MY BEAUTY AND IN MY GOODNESS
I CAME TO KNOW MY SELF AND LOVE WHAT I FOUND THERE.

I MADE PEACE WITH MY SELF
AND SAW THE GOOD IN ME AND IN OTHERS.
I LEARNED SELF-RESPECT AND SO I RESPECT OTHERS
I BELIEVE IN MY IDEAS, MY WANTS, AND DESIRES
AND WATCH MY DREAMS COME TRUE.

I HELPED MY SELF AND THEN I COULD HELP OTHERS.
I TURNED OFF THE TAPES, COMMANDS, DIRECTIONS,
AND INSTRUCTIONS TO BELIEVE IN
OTHER THINGS AND OTHER PEOPLE
AND LISTENED TO MY HEART
AND I ALLOWED OTHERS TO LISTEN TO THEIRS.

I AM ME AND I WILL ENJOY IT ALWAYS
AND I AM BEGINNING TO CONCEIVE OF MY OTHER HALF
MY SOUL MATE, MY HIM.

THE MIST IS BEGINNING TO CLEAR,
I SEE HIM IN THE DISTANCE, A VAGUE OUTLINE STILL
I FEEL HIM IN MY HEART
I AM HERE AND HE WILL COME
I AM HAPPY.

--DINI PETTY

Dini's Personal Self-Directed Journey

I wrote this poem in November of 1995 just after my life started to change. My longtime companion of low Self-esteem was disappearing and high Self-esteem was moving in. It had been a lifelong struggle.

I never learned I was supposed to like my Self. I always thought I had to be liked by everyone else. So I spent a great part of my life watching others react to me, trying to figure out if they liked me or not. I tried to please so many different people--my father, for example, who criticized and corrected me, I think he believed it would make me better. As a child, my interpretation of this helpful criticism was that I was never quite good enough. Fortunately, I also learned from him that I could do anything if I put my mind to it and applied my Self. I heard him say it would take an awful lot of hard work, but if I persisted I would win.

As a result, I grew up believing I was able to do anything if I applied my Self, but also thinking I would never be good enough.

When I was in my 20's, I learned to fly helicopters. It was complicated and it took me awhile, but I persisted. When I got it all together I did the traffic reports while flying, sipping coffee, talking on the intercom to my passenger, talking to the other helicopters, the towers, and the operators at the station. I learned to do all of it and because I was the only female in an all-male world, I learned to be damn good at it.

When I thought about it, though, I always believed that they'd fire me because I wasn't good enough. Never being good enough, or at least believing that to be the case, took a lot out of what I had accomplished. I never really spent much time enjoying what I was doing, or being proud and congratulating my Self because I knew that if I had only done this or that, then maybe, just maybe, I would be good enough.

From my mother I received an all-in-one lesson on kindness, gentleness, beauty, and brains. She was well travelled as a child, spending time in Kenya, East Africa. She learned Swahili, which I thought sounded amazing. Africa has since become one of my favourite places to go. She served in British intelligence in WWII and went on to raise a family and run a successful talent agency, which is where I got my start. I am like my mother in so many ways, except I learned to like my Self.

I believe that if my mother had known that she was supposed to like her Self and had seen her Self as the beautiful, dynamic, intelligent, and extraordinarily successful woman that she was, it would have prevented her from becoming an alcoholic. A condition that took so much of her life and happiness, in fact, it almost killed her. But after spending three days in her third coma mother woke up and finally decided that she had a drinking problem and, on her own, quit drinking.

I accept the destiny she chose, and allow my Self mine, and get on with the lessons of truly loving and respecting my Self so I continue to feel happy. As a result of putting my Self first, I enjoy being with my mate, children, family members, and my real friends so much more.

Putting my Self first has been one of my greatest lessons. Growing up I learned that it was important to be liked by others and to please others, and that my needs were secondary. I learned that living my life for my Self was selfish and greedy and that only by living my life for others would I be happy. I did that for many years. But eventually I learned that until I was happy with me, listened to my heart, and spoke only the truth to my Self, could I be truly happy. I waited a long time to feel these things; the things I wish someone had explained and demonstrated to me as a child.

How different my life would have been, how much hurt I could have avoided if this had been the case. I got so lost in other things and other people. I used so much time and energy.

I believed it was important to live in the best of homes, eat at the best of places, and associate with the best people. I thought it was important to wear mink coats and diamonds. Dini Petty, celebrity socialite. I lived like this for a long time and I was pretty good at it. The fact that I was miserable inside seemed unimportant.

By my own definition of what I thought I should be, I should have been very happy. Yet something was missing and I could never figure out what it was. I looked for the answer in so many places and for so many years and did find many answers yet I still felt incomplete. My career has been my saving grace; flying helicopters, anchoring television news, and hosting talk shows introduced me to thousands of people from many different places and I learned and grew from these experiences. Still there was always something lacking. Eventually I grew weary of searching and accepted that this was how my life would be. I was ready to accept the fact that I'd never find my personal happiness and my own peace of mind. And just about the time I was ready to give up, I met Sandra Harding and began my Self-Directed Journey.

The first change I consciously made was to understand that how I thought about my Self and how I treated my Self was the root of my problem. This combined with a few other things like putting everyone else first (what I call an Out/In perspective), ignoring my instinct, and forgetting about the essential basics (food, water, and rest), amounted to my unhappiness.

I have watched many others walk this same path. I have seen lives altered and watched dreams come true because people got in touch with their instinct and followed their own truths.

When Sandy asked me to speak about Self-Direction the timing was right. I had been working in the Third World Aid scene for several years when I realized that I wanted to invest more of my time in my own country. I decided to speak on this particular subject because I realized that before I could truly help others, it was first necessary to help my Self.

I have been making a speech to students of all ages, as well as men and women across Canada, for the last two years. This book parallels the topics in the speech. I enjoy doing it and receiving feedback from those who have heard it.

This journey builds awareness; do it your own way, and at your own pace. The principles and insights into Instinct, Self-Confidence, Self-Esteem and Processing In/Out presented in this journey make life better because they encourage the development of your Self-authority. I have observed that younger people get it faster. I think it is because they have carried their own personal baggage for much less time.

Had I known these things in my youth, how different the quality of my life would have been. But I know these things now and that's what counts.

Dini Petty

A Self-Directed Journey

A Self-Directed Journey is a process whereby we learn to be aware of our instinct and use our intellect to select actions that help us direct our lives. In short, it is learning to trust our Self and our judgments.

We define the Self as the source of all new options and perceptions. We believe Self is our soul. Self is the part of us that knows what is best for us and instinct is the messenger of Self. This makes instinct the boss.

Whenever we actively encourage our instinct to have its proper role as boss, the dynamics of how we do things changes. At times, this forces us to face certain truths. Although it may be unfamiliar at first, people who have worked through the process are always glad they did. We have profiled some people of all ages, who are making this journey and have included their feedback to give you an idea of other people's experiences as well as ours.

The butterfly symbolizes the Self-Directed Journey because it represents the process of discovering and working with our nature...our true Self. Just as a caterpillar transforms itself into a butterfly, we, too, can use our Self to reorganize the relationship between instinct, intellect, body, and mind and make our lives much better.

HOW TO USE THIS BOOK

This book has been designed in four parts, each corresponding to one stage of the butterfly's development into maturity. Within each part, there is an introduction and five lessons, one for each of the five categories used in the Self-Directed Learning system. These categories are the areas that fulfill the Self-preservation needs of our instinct. They are:

- HEALTH
- RELATIONSHIPS
- LEARNING
- LANGUAGE
- TIME MANAGEMENT

The main text and lessons are on the right side of the pages. These offer interesting perspectives, techniques, real life examples, and Self-Directed profiles to help develop instinct as leader and ensure that you are working for the fulfillment of your personal goals. They are part of the ingredients for getting what you want from your Self and your world. After each section and at the end of the book, there is space to record your personal insights. On the left side of the pages are stories and quotes for inspiration and reflection. There is also more space here for you to write your thoughts. We suggest after reading each lesson, you write in your own words what the lesson means to you and where to apply it. Doing this, personalizes the lesson and makes it Self-Directed.

We recommend that you do your best to apply the principles and techniques as you learn them, with a light-hearted attitude.

Instinct AND *Self-Preservation*

*T*HE FIRST STAGE IN THE DEVELOPMENT

OF THE BUTTERFLY IS THE EGG PHASE.

THIS IS WHERE THE IDEA TO USE SELF-DIRECTION

IS BORN AND BEGINS TO GROW.

*Once my Self-preservation needs are met,
the door to prosperity opens.*

-- SANDRA HARDING

Instinct and Self-Preservation

GOOD HEALTH
IS THE FOUNDATION OF PROSPERITY

The most important ingredient in good health is to understand the value of getting in touch with and following our instinct. Instinct is related to fear. The more we listen to and follow our instinct, the less fear we have. The more we argue with and ignore our instinct, the more fearful we become. To quiet fear, it is important to become more instinctive. Below are the three principles which enable us to easily access our instinct:

1. **Fill up, then do.** It is essential to fill up with the basics everyday, all day. These are food, water, and rest. We have to fill up our tank so that we can produce the energy needed to do the things we want to do in a day.

2. **My Self, then you.** We have to satisfy our own safety and survival needs first before we can focus on helping others fulfill theirs. Otherwise, our own energy is drained and we develop resentful feelings.

3. **I focus on what I want.** Wherever instinct directs us, our mind will take us. To focus on what we want builds energy. When we focus on what we don't want, energy is wasted.

REMEMBER:

Fill up, then do
My Self, then you
and
I focus on what I want

> *Self-esteem is being in a body that is reflective of respect for food, water and rest. The basic ingredients of Self-Directed living.*

-- BRIAN

There are two parts to our instinct *(see Figure 1)*. The first part is our Self-preservation reflex and the second is our prosperity builder. Before we can get into prosperity-building mode, there is an automatic prioritization that occurs in our instinct which ensures our survival needs are met first.

DOING THE BASICS

Many people struggle everyday because they fail to fulfill the basic survival requirements needed to satisfy their Self-preservation. These basic ingredients are:
1. Food: eating well
2. Water: drinking enough
3. Rest and relaxation: proper sleep and time for Self

Once these needs are fulfilled, we automatically move towards a prosperous frame of mind, creating a positive and optimistic internal dialogue. Our thoughts become calm, collected, and constructive.

The bottom line is that we have to fulfill our survival needs for food, water, and rest before we can initiate a prosperity-building mode and feel satisfied with our Self. Only then are we naturally motivated and nourished by helping others.

This shift from survival mode to prosperity-building mode is a fundamental part of human nature and is the backbone of life.

Mornings were always frantic for me.
I would wake feeling anxious and tired.
Before my feet even hit the ground my thoughts
were on waking and feeding my son and husband.
I would put their needs first, get them out the door
to school and work, then I would tend to my Self.

I began to feel put upon and resentful.
Through Self-Directed Learning, I learned
to do the basics (food, water, rest) for me first.
My morning routine takes the same amount
of time as before except the order in which I do things
is different. Now I tend to my needs first.
This routine ensures that I am properly nurtured.

I am now calm and happy in the mornings
and I receive great pleasure from seeing
my family rested, nourished and content.

-- KATHY

Our instinct is our primary Self-Directing force. For me, I feel my instinct in my heart. When something is good for me, my heart feels calm and relaxed. When something, someone, or some situation is negative for me my heart tenses up and I feel uncomfortable.

Instinct works differently for everybody. Dini feels her's in her gut. Everyone feels instinct in his/her own unique place. It could be in their gut, stomach, heart, or head. It could be anywhere. It could be a voice that gives a definite "Yes" or "No." However it works for you, it is yours to figure out.

An interesting way to get in touch with your instinct is to draw a picture of what your instinct looks like.

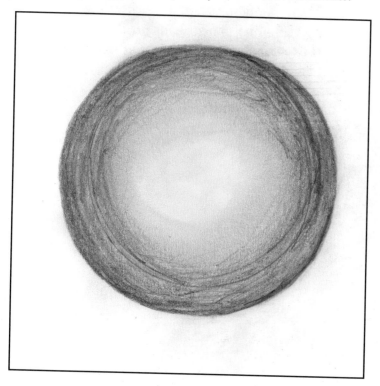

> *Doing the basics is essential*
> *in order to hear your instinct.*
> *If you ignore this, you might as well stop*
> *your Self-Directed Journey now —*
> *you want to struggle in life.*

-- SANDRA HARDING

THE TWO PARTS OF INSTINCT

PROSPERITY BUILDER
(Builds Understanding)

SELF-PRESERVATION
(Quiets Fear)

INSTINCT
(SELF)

OUR INSTINCT MAKES SURE OUR SELF-PRESERVATION NEEDS ARE MET FIRST BEFORE WE GET INTO PROSPERITY-BUILDING MODE. THIS QUIETS FEAR AND BUILDS UNDERSTANDING.

The Path of the Butterfly

THE THOUGHT IS BORN INSIDE
IT IS THEN A DREAM
THE DREAMER LEARNS TO BELIEVE IN HER SELF
AND LISTENS TO HER THOUGHTS UNTIL
SHE HEARS HER FULL SELF
AND THERE SHE WATCHES AS HER DREAMS COME TRUE
AND THERE SHE LEARNS OF COURAGE AS SHE WALKS
HER OWN PATH
HER OWN WAY
AND LISTENS TO NEITHER THE PRAISE NOR THE CRITICISM
BUT LISTENS TO HER OWN HEART
AND FINALLY REALIZES HER OWN DESTINY.

--DINI PETTY

Instinct and Self-Preservation
LESSON 1 : HEALTH

Fast pace living and putting other things before our health needs has caused our Self-preservation reflex to be over active. Things that are minor become major. We overreact. An example is road rage. Leave late, no time to eat, grab a coffee, yell. The first step in building health is to quiet heightened Self-preservation reflex.

Putting our health needs first does this. This satisfies our nourishment needs. This is the only way to keep our Self-preservation reflex calm, move forward easily, and build our health and vitality.

To get in touch with your nourishment needs, rate your Self on the following statements, with 1 as low and 5 being high:

Statement	1	2	3	4	5	
I eat well	1	(2)	3	4	5	
I drink enough water	1	2	(3)	4	5	
I sleep enough	1	2	(3)	4	5	
I have enough leisure time	1	(2)	3	4	5	(11)
I put my needs first	(1)	2	3	4	5	

Add up the numbers. If they are less than 20, list some of the things you can do to improve your score.

This is Sandra's sample schedule that she used to learn good eating habits:

Sample schedule
- *Breakfast*   *7:30 a.m.*
- *Lunch*   *12:00 p.m.*
- *Afternoon snack*   *2:15 p.m. and 4:30 p.m.*
- *Dinner*   *6:00 p.m.*
- *Evening snack*   *9:00 p.m.*
- *3 glasses of water a day and in bed at 11:30 p.m.*

An example of Sandra's daily nourishment needs now are:
- *A light breakfast with fruit, protein, toast, coffee, water.*
- *For lunch, a sandwich with protein, vegetables, and a can of pop.*
- *A snack when she wants, with some water.*
- *A full dinner consisting of proteins and vegetables or carbohydrates and vegetables, with a little wine and dessert.*

*When I prepare food for others in the morning,
I make sure that I've eaten
something before I feed them.*

--SANDRA HARDING

Write a description of your daily nourishment needs:

Food: _____

Water: _____

Rest and Sleep: _____

Play: _____

I used to argue with my Self
and take it out on others.
After the fact I realized that it had more to do
with my low Self-esteem than anything
anyone had done or said.
Over time, I learned to tune into my instinct
and took the time to understand my position
from a high Self-esteem perspective
before I communicated with others.
As a result, I am more positive in my dealings
with my Self, my husband, family, and friends.
I have learned to enjoy
my relationships more.

--RENÉE

Instinct and Self-Preservation

LESSON 2: RELATIONSHIPS

It is important to develop a strong and healthy relationship with our instinct. Every person has their own thoughts and feelings about the attention they want to receive from their mate, children, friends, and others. What we get from others is determined by the relationship we have with our Self and the way we interpret our instinct.

It is natural for our instinct to direct us in our day-to-day decisions. The only reason we lose touch or ignore our instinct is because we learned that others know what is better for us than we know for our Self. We take our focus off our Self and our needs and put it on them and their needs. When this happens, our Self-preservation reflex goes into survival mode.

We make our best decisions when we stay in touch with our instinct and keep our focus on our Self and our needs. This develops our Self-Directing abilities and builds our prosperity. We can have faith in our judgment to exercise our Self-authority. In time, using instinct to lead in decision making becomes automatic and a good habit. The following exercise helps us get in touch with the difference between going with our instinct and ignoring our instinct.

Every day I do the basics, set my goals,
focus on what I am doing
and appreciate what I have.
Some days, I spend time releasing old muscle
memories and clutter from my psyche.
Because I do these things,
I keep my relationship with my Self
strong, healthy, and vibrant.

-- SANDRA HARDING

Recall a time when you ignored your instinct.
Think about that time and remember how everything
turned out. Describe the situation.

> *When I work instinctively,*
> *I have a quiet mind and maintain focus*
> *from start to finish.*

-- MICHAEL

Recall a time when you went with your instinct.
How did things turn out? Describe the situation.

> *When I am out of balance I feel my feet on the floor and listen to my breathing for one minute.*

--SANDRA HARDING

Instinct and Self-Preservation

LESSON 3: LEARNING

Learning how to deal with stress, tension, and emotional baggage is a very important part of quieting one's inner struggle and opening the door to prosperity. The following are two techniques we have found useful to keep an open channel to our instinct. We named them Muscle Memory Release and Mental Trash Elimination.

The Muscle Memory Release technique is an exercise to balance tension in our muscles, particularly in the pericardium muscle and in our heart. The pericardium is a sac of muscle surrounding the heart. The heart works with the pericardium to pump blood through our body. When we get tense, our heart has to work harder. Whenever our thinking is stressed, our heart is distressed. It is necessary to release the tension.

To Muscle Memory Release:

• Lay on your back and put your hands straight up over your head.

• Imagine your Self feeling relaxed and pick a colour.

• Imagine breathing in that colour and stretch like you are trying to grow, pushing out with your heels first then pointing your toes. Once you have stretched as far as you can, exhale your colour with a sigh, and relax.

This technique helps to balance your stress, because it distributes the tension and stress equally throughout your body. Doing this exercise three times in the morning and three times at night is a good way to keep balanced.

By getting my mental crap down on paper,
I remove the clutter
so I can have an organized mind.

--DINI PETTY

The Muscle Memory Release technique can also be done standing up. To do this:

• Plant your feet securely on the floor.

• Imagine your Self feeling relaxed and pick a colour.

• Imagine breathing in that colour while stretching as tall as you can, while pushing your feet down into the ground. Then, spring up on the balls of your feet and come back down as you exhale your colour with a sigh and relax.

The second technique, Mental Trash Elimination, works well to quiet mental chatter and settle emotions. When we become flustered and confused in our thinking, we sometimes focus more on our negative Self-images and belittling thoughts. When this happens, get it out of your system by writing these thoughts down. If you use scrap paper to spew on, you can tear it up, throw it away, or recycle it.

Both techniques help keep our instinct in prosperity mode. The first technique covers the physical issues, the second mental and emotional triggers.

We have found the best way to use the past constructively is to learn from our experiences. By doing this, we make their meanings positive and end up valuing them. In this way the past can become part of the richness of the present, rather than interfering with our enjoyment of it.

Most of us have been conditioned to focus on where we are going or where we have been, but rarely where we are right now. By learning to have our mind on what we are doing in the present, we put our instinct in touch with our action. This places us in the correct frame of mind to learn and do things to the best of our ability. The advantages of this are increased awareness, good focus, improved safety and efficient use of time.

Kathy - Learning to hear and follow my instinct has taught me to listen with the intent to learn rather than with the intent to respond. I have learned to focus in the present.

Here are three suggestions to help you practice
focusing in the present:

1. While eating, focus on what you are eating.
   Notice the smells, colours, tastes, and textures.

2. While driving, focus on driving and where you are.

3. While walking, focus on feeling the sidewalk under
   your feet.

   Make up a few of your own suggestions on things you
   can do to practice focusing in the present:

I know I am in tune with my instinct
when I can focus where I am.

-- SANDRA HARDING

Write about being in the present.

Pam - When I'm tuned in to my instinct, I go at my own pace and focus in the present. I am aware of the language I use.

Instinct and Self-Preservation

LESSON 4: LANGUAGE

Our language is an automatic behaviour that we have developed from our experiences in life. It is important to have a language which enables and encourages us to put our Self first, and prioritize our needs.

There are two kinds of language. "I can do it" language, and "I can't do it" language. When we are in our "I can do it" language, we are naturally motivated to fulfill our basic wants and needs and are ready to move forward. The "I can't do it" language triggers doubt and Self-defeating thoughts, so we ignore our basic needs and waste a lot of energy struggling with our Self.

Emotions are our inner response to our own language. By nourishing our Self and using "I can do it" language, we create balanced emotions. It's a way to keep our language in prosperity mode.

*When I focus on what I can do,
I feel satisfied with what I have
and I am happier in general.*

-- MICHAEL

Write a list of things you want to do better.

When I feel short of time and scattered,
I'm usually thirsty.

-- SANDRA HARDING

Instinct and Self-Preservation

LESSON 5: TIME MANAGEMENT

Instinct is in charge of time management and knows when we need to eat, sleep, play, and work. Instinct naturally prioritizes our health and well-being as most important and lets us know when one of our basic needs requires attention. We can either listen to it or ignore this message. If we ignore the message from our instinct, our perception focuses on problems rather than solutions. We struggle with our time management.

If this happens, take a moment and ask your Self which of the basics do I need? Wait for an answer and do it. Taking this time out puts us back in touch with our instinct.

Here is a list to help identify which of the basics to use:

- If you feel anxious, worried, intimidated, drink more water.

- If you are tired or your energy drops, eat some food.

- If you are angry, short-fused and over-reacting, get some rest.

- If you are tense....deep breathe.

A glass of water is enough. A handful of nuts will do and sitting down for one minute and taking a few deep breaths counts as rest.

*I use my instinct all the time.
The more I use it, the easier it gets.*

--DINI PETTY

Self-Directed Profiles

Where has learning to hear and follow your instinct made your life easier?

Pam - I can stop second guessing my Self. Positive things fill my life. I have confidence and high Self-esteem. This all comes from being able to hear and follow my instinct.

Kathy - Learning to hear and follow my instinct has made my life easier because now I argue less with my Self. This results in the coordination of how I feel, how I think and what I do. This internal alignment keeps me quiet inside, ensuring that I am safe and get what I want. I hear my Self, I listen to my Self, and I take direction from my Self. Therefore, I create a safe environment for me to get what I want and need.

Michelle - I try to solve all my problems first before turning to others for support. I feel much more independent.

Gitte - Now that I hear my instinct my life is simple. I imagine my Self, my instinct, surrounded by rings of colour protecting and helping me to evolve to a higher level of consciousness. I love my Self and the way I am now.

Lynda - I can now be more focused on my direction in life. I take responsibility for the things that are happening on a day-to-day basis. It is easier to do that when I listen to my instinct because more and more I like what is happening.

What I get from Self-Directed Learning
is the confidence
to exercise my Self-authority.

-- KORBY

Instinct

Main ingredient:

Use the basics.

This is the best way to put your
Self first, tuning into and developing
a relationship with your instinct.

Frequently Asked Questions

When I have a decision to make how do I know which option is my instinct's?

Instinct is directly connected to health. Whatever decision I make that is best for my health is the correct instinct.

Imagine your Self in each scenario. The one that quiets internal argument is the one that is good for health. The one you feel motivated to do.

Is putting my Self and my needs first selfish?

No. We are encouraging you to put your health needs first. The basics. It is our instinctive nature to put our Self and health first. It is the key to prosperity.

Write to Make Right

_____

_____

_____

_____

_____

_____

_____

_____

_____

_____

_____

_____

_____

*"When I write about something,
I can make it right for me."* -- SANDRA HARDING

Instinct AND Self-Confidence

THE SECOND STAGE IN THE DEVELOPMENT

OF THE BUTTERFLY IS THE CATERPILLAR (LARVA) STAGE.

THIS IS WHERE THE GROWING SELF-DIRECTION

BUILDS SELF-CONFIDENCE.

As a clothing designer, I am asked to be out there
to provide clothing for people to wear
that are also out there.
Being out there requires confidence.
It requires Self-Direction.

-- BRIAN

Instinct and Self-Confidence

Self-confidence is the second stage of the Self-Directed Journey. Self-confidence occurs when we know we can do something well. There are two steps to knowing we can do this. The first is how well we have learned to do something. The second is how well we apply and refine what we have learned to do. This development of what we have learned to do is the job of our instinct and intellect working together. When we let our instinct lead, we refine our skills over time. This is the Self-confidence that comes from being able to Self-Direct. When we are Self-confident we enter new situations feeling comfortable. If we are out of touch with our instinct, we are uncomfortable entering new situations and this limits our personal development.

This is true for present situations. For example, if a problem comes up and we are in touch with our instinct, we feel confident in our ability to solve it. However, if we are out of touch with our instinct, we feel intimidated by the problem because we have no direction from our instinct. Simply put, we don't know what to do, and we give the problem our power.

The common result of increased Self-confidence is a stronger belief in Self so that we can learn and then accomplish what we set out to do. Being in touch with and learning from instinct is the backbone of Self-confidence.

As in the **Instinct and Self-preservation** section, there are five lessons. These show you how to develop Self-confidence so that you can feel comfortable with your Self and others in the same five areas of your life.

Lynda - *I can take charge of my health and make choices about being healthy. When I do get ill I heal quicker and with more confidence.*

Instinct and Self-Confidence

LESSON 1: HEALTH

When we analyse our health, it is our instinct that informs us if anything needs to be done. If we notice we feel tired and achy, we get an idea of what the problem is and what to do to remedy the situation. For example, consider more sleep, more food, some medicine, or time for our Self. Self-confidence helps us believe we are capable of deciding on an action to make us feel better.

Often, however, making health decisions is difficult because most of us have learned that a good person puts another before him or her Self. We look to outside sources as authority and our attention is outside of our Self, instead of on our Self. In order to build Self-confidence to direct and manage health, we must prioritize our Self first and have our mind on our instinct.

It is important to recycle the old habit of caring more about other people than we do for our Self. The trouble with caring more about others is that it goes against our own Self-preservation and triggers anger in us because we are neglecting our responsibilities to our Self. A way to remember to put our Self first is to use this affirmation:

Take only *my* problems to heart.

I learned what to do from my instinct, then I became Self-confident that I knew what to do for my own health needs.

-- MICHAEL

Taking others' problems to heart causes a lot of needless worry. Taking our own problems to heart gives natural priority to situations in our health and life. Once personal problems are solved, then we can gladly lend our support to help others solve their own problems.

Recall a time when you knew what to do
for your health and it worked.

*Giving to Self and receiving from Self
is the original give-and-take relationship
on which all other relationships are based.
Depending on how this one works decides
what kind of relationships we attract.*

-- SANDRA HARDING

Instinct and Self-Confidence

LESSON 2: RELATIONSHIPS

All day we are receiving from Self and giving to Self. We define Self as the source of all new options and perceptions. Therefore, if we feel insecure we have to receive confidence from our Self. If we feel tired we have to receive energy from our Self. If we would like to see things differently, or find new ways of experiencing things, we have to receive the new options for this from our Self. It's safe to say that our Self contains the catalogue where we can go shopping to choose how we wish to interpret our Self in the world.

Giving to Self is a different story. We give to our Self when we do the basics: food, water, rest. This encourages the use of our instinct. We give to our Self when we pamper our Self, such as when we have a good workout, take a warm bath, or just enjoy absorbing our spirit. We give to our Self when we spend time enjoying our family and playing. In return, we receive from our Self many positive feelings from these experiences.

Giving to Self and receiving from Self is the original give-and-take relationship. The idea is to use our instinct and intellect to find the unique balance in knowing when to give to our Self and when to take from our Self. Having this knowledge creates confidence. When we have balance in our relationship to our Self, we can then feel confident in knowing that we will attract good quality relationships with others.

> *Since I started my Self-Directed Journey, I have received my sense of purpose from my Self.*

-- RENÉE

Write what you want to receive from your Self.

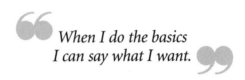

*When I do the basics
I can say what I want.*

-- SANDRA HARDING

Get in touch with your instinctive relationship desires.
List the things you would like (where they apply)
in your relationships with:

your Self: _____

your mate : _____

your children: _____

your friends : _____

your work: _____

My favourite gift to me is time;
time with my Self to write, to draw,
to read in bed. Time for a great workout.
Time for a bath with essential oils and candles.
The gift of doing these things
when I want to. That's luxury!

-- DINI PETTY

Now write out the things you want to give to your Self.

"I used to have trouble spelling words and remembering how to use capitals and punctuations. Through my lessons in Self-Directed Learning, I learned to imagine I can spell my words right and remember to use capitals and punctuations.

Now I take my time, stay still and stay focused. I am doing better on tests and my writing is neater."

--SHAUN

Instinct and Self-Confidence

LESSON 3: LEARNING

In order for us to learn easily, we need to be in touch with our instinct and focus on what we want to learn. This is done by using our foresight. Foresight is the picture we put into our head. We can either use "What I want" foresight or "What I don't want" foresight. "What I want" foresight builds Self-confidence. "What I don't want" foresight works to get us what we don't want and weaken Self-confidence. Therefore, whenever we endeavour to learn something, it is very important to imagine that we can do it and to set a goal of what we want.

Foreseeing what we want and working to experience it is a vital part of successful learning and doing. Here is an example: Sally is standing on the eighth tee at the local golf course. Her friend Ralph approaches the tee. His swing has sent his golf ball sailing into the water hazard left of the fairway. Immediately, Sally thinks to her Self, "I don't want my ball to go into the water!" This puts Sally's foresight to work because by putting a picture in her mind of her hitting the ball into the water, her mind works towards that goal. And sure enough her shot ends up in the water.

This is an example of "what I don't want" foresight. It would have been better for Sally to have put the picture in her head of hitting the ball onto the fairway. This puts the "What I want" foresight to work and her mind will work towards that. Using foresight this way builds Self-confidence and enables us to learn and do things the best we can.

*Managing money and number crunching
were always a weakness of mine.
Often my emotions were governed
by my financial status.
I worried that I never saved money,
that I spent too much,
and that my child didn't appreciate
the value of money.*

*When I learned to hear and follow my instinct,
I trusted my ability to learn what I needed to know
about financial planning.
Now when I think, "What if I can't do it?",
or, "What if I don't understand it?",
I flush these thoughts, organize my Self,
and do more research.*

*The knowledge I gain from doing more research helps
to calm my fear of failure. My Self-confidence is
enhanced because now I feel "I can do it!"
I am my own authority over my money.
I manage it, save it, invest it, and spend what I want.
My ten year old son receives a weekly allowance.
He has opened a bank account and
I see him understanding the value of money.
I see him managing his own
money with confidence.*

--KATHY

When learning something, it is important to foresee what you want to achieve. Using your "What I want" foresight, write about two things you are currently working on and describe the picture in your mind of what you want to achieve.

Pam - *My language is much more positive.*
I say what I want.

Instinct and Self-Confidence

LESSON 4: LANGUAGE

It is important to be aware of the language we use to our Self. The language we use affects our health and Self-confidence. For example, the old expression, "You make me sick." This is typical of a mixed message. The truth is that how I perceive what you are doing makes me feel sick. So how we structure our language can make us feel victimized. However in reality, you didn't do it to me. I did it to my Self by how I perceived you. Therefore, it is necessary to choose how we perceive people and things around us so that we can feel confident. Here are more examples of negative language:

• "I can't stand it."	**This is a way to make your back hurt.**
• "I'm sick and tired of this."	**Therefore, this is what you will be.**
• "I'm dying to do that."	**Why? What a waste.**
• "I don't believe it."	**If it's a good thing, it's better to believe it.**

And here are other phrases we often hear that can say a lot about people's perception and how they undermine their Self-confidence:

- "I'm so stupid."
- "I'm such an idiot."
- "I'm such a loser."
- "How dumb of me."
- "I'm sorry, I'm sorry..."   **(How many times a day do we hear or use this phrase?!)**

*My dreams are right for me
providing I include me in my
picture and my language to me.
To manifest what is right for me,
I must write my words and
pictures with me in mind.*

-- SANDRA HARDING

It is easy to see from these examples that a demeaning language built upon negativity takes away from Self-confidence. Listen to the language that you use about your Self, your friends, and your family. Listen to the language of others. It's amazing how some of us describe our Self.

Here are several language phrases to consider using that build up Self-confidence:

- "I can deal with it."
- "I need a break."
- "I really want to do that."
- "I believe it."
- "Oops, I want to try that again."
- "I can do it."
- "I'm so clever."
- "I'm amazed."

It is very important to be aware of our language so that we can use it to build up our Self-confidence and describe what we want instead of Self-bashing.

Write some phrases of your own that build you up.

Lynda - *I procrastinate less. I get on with the job. I focus on what I accomplish and I am punctual.*

Instinct and Self-Confidence

LESSON 5: TIME MANAGEMENT

When we follow our instinct, we feel confident we are using our time wisely. With this security, we can focus on what we accomplish each day. Focusing on what we accomplish each day is a good way to boost our energy level. We derive nourishment from what we do, as well as feel the rewards of our achievement. In this way we can get pleasure from our work.

If we focus on what we don't accomplish each day, we will build apathy and kill our motivation.

Focusing on what we accomplish is nourishing to our Self and is an easy way to maintain our motivation. The more we get done, the bigger our feeling of satisfaction and the more we want to do. This naturally creates an "I can do it" language and "what I want" foresight.

"I can do it" language and "what I want" foresight keep us focused on what we are doing and we get the most out of our time in productivity and nourishment. We feel more confident managing our time and learn to trust our instinct.

If people set out to accomplish
ten things in their day, but only nine
of them get done,
why is it that they focus on that tenth one
and think they had a lousy day
rather than enjoy the nine
accomplishments they did have?

-- DINI PETTY

Self-Directed Profiles

Where has learning to hear and follow your instinct affected your Self-confidence?

Pam — Learning to hear and follow my instinct has boosted my Self-confidence in all that I do.

Kathy — Learning to hear and follow my instinct has enhanced my Self-confidence because as I've learned to remain calm and quiet inside, my fear of failure and the "What if I can't do it" thoughts are quiet as well. Through Self-Direction I have acquired the ability to flush negative thoughts and organize the positive ones, so that I can approach daily tasks and challenges with a quiet confidence in my ability to do it and learn how to do it.

Michelle — After making some decisions on your own (ones in which you would normally seek support), you start to believe in your Self more than ever and that definitely builds your Self-confidence.

Gitte — I know consciously and intuitively that I can do anything I want to do. That is Self-confidence. In the past year I pushed my Self to the edge and because of my absolute belief in my instinct, I healed my Self back to a balanced life through colour imagery, healing meditation, and positive thinking.

Lynda — I am and have always been Self-confident. Becoming Self-Directed has helped me feel good about that Self-confidence.

I do Believe

I remember when things started to change for Dini.
I would receive voice-mail that started with,
"I can't believe it!" Following that she would
inform me of something really good happening,
something she had wanted for a long time.
My response to her was, "When something good
happens, receive it by saying, I do believe."
This way you welcome your wish come true.
The next call I wish I could have framed
because Dini started it with,
"I do believe! I do believe! I do believe!"
It was wonderful music to my ears.

-- SANDRA HARDING

Self-confidence

Main ingredient:

Prioritize having instinct lead your decisions so it becomes familiar. Believe in your Self-Direction to build an attitude of confidence.

Write to Make Right

_____

_____

_____

_____

_____

_____

_____

_____

_____

_____

_____

_____

_____

_____

"When I write about something,
I can make it right for me." -- SANDRA HARDING

Instinct AND
Self-Esteem

*T*HE THIRD STAGE IN THE TRANSFORMATION
OF THE BUTTERFLY IS THE PUPA OR CHRYSALIS PHASE.
THIS IS WHERE THE DEVELOPMENT OF THE IDEA
TO FUNCTION SELF-DIRECTED MATURES WITHIN.

> *Low Self-esteem is a plague on the land*
> *that we must heal.*
> *We owe it to our Self and our children.*

-- DINI PETTY

At this point in the Self-Directed Journey, we have learned how to open a clear channel to our instinct by doing the basics everyday. We have also learned that how well we hear and follow our instinct determines our confidence level. "I can do it" language builds Self-confidence, and Self-confidence enables us to increase our Self-value and what we think we deserve. We then develop thoughts and a language of high Self-esteem. It's a cycle that builds on itself.

Self-esteem is how we think about our Self inside. Self-esteem directly affects our personal energy and motivation. If we think about our Self in a respectful and constructive way, then our energy level and motivation increases. If we think about our Self in a negative and disrespectful way, then our energy level and motivation decreases. The goal is to find a place where our Self-esteem helps maintain our energy level and motivation.

"Kind to Self" language is one way we create and build high Self-esteem. Our language is made from our thoughts. When our thoughts are positive and good, then our language is constructive.

To understand the problem with the "I can't do it" or "I'm never good enough" language is to realize that most of us learned a language of negative Self-esteem. We were often judged and questioned about our choice of actions. We learned to look for what was wrong and out of place. In school and at home, the focus was often on what we did wrong more than what we did right.

I use to focus on avoiding problems
but this used too much energy.
Now I focus on where I want to go.

--MICHAEL

As a result, we placed too much focus on our perceived weaknesses. Focusing on what's wrong wastes a lot of energy. Our mind gets the message that "what we don't want" is, in fact, what we do want. We interpret our instinct dyslexically, and we end up with what we don't want. It is like telling a child "Don't touch that." What do you think will happen? Of course, often, they will touch it.

We have all met people who can tell us everything they don't want and yet have no clue what they do want. These same people are good at noticing what they didn't get done in their day rather than what they have accomplished. People who perceive like this, usually notice what is wrong rather than what is right and focus on avoidance of failure instead of what can be learned.

The next five lessons will help you build your Self-esteem by shifting the focus from what's wrong to what's right using "kind to Self" language and focusing on accomplishments.

The statements below are high Self-esteem attitudes.

- I know what I want.
- I value hearing and following my instinct.
- I make time to relax.
- I know how much to sleep, I wake up
  rested and energized.
- I think constructively with optimism.
- I react appropriately and I am balanced.
- I deal with situations objectively.
- I can do it.

I used to think in terms of
what I didn't want to happen to me.
Now that I'm working with my instinct,
I think in terms of what I want.
I use my instinct to point me in the direction
to get the advice I need from my Self
and from others to get there.

-- RENÉE

Make a list of the things that you don't want or
that you think are *wrong* with your life.

Michelle - *Thinking within brings out the beauty within -- the beauty of being my own person, making decisions, and solving problems.*

List some things that build up your Self-esteem:

> *How I think about my Self*
> *affects how the world*
> *thinks of me.*

-- MATTHEW

Now make a list of the things that you think
you want in your life.

Pam - *I am beautiful, regardless of physical size. People notice size only when I feel Self-conscious or have low Self-esteem thoughts about size.*

For so many of us the list of what is wrong comes easily relative to the list of what we like about our life. This is a sign of low Self-esteem.

When you find your Self-esteem is slipping, place your focus on the second and third list to remind you to value and respect your Self.

Kathy - Learning to hear and follow my instinct has improved my health immensely. Now I put my Self first. I exercise my mind through writing, my body through physical exercise, and my soul through Self-love. I feel strong and healthy.

Instinct and Self-Esteem

LESSON 1: HEALTH

High Self-esteem is a very important element of good health. When we value hearing and following our instinct, it builds Self-confidence. This enables us to achieve our goals, which builds our Self-esteem. Self-esteem is the thermostat of personal energy, so when we build our Self-esteem, our energy increases. In other words, maintaining high Self-esteem helps maintain a high energy level.

Over time, this leads to a personal energy surplus which can be defined as, "I make more energy than I use each day." It is natural to feel positive about our Self when we have a surplus of personal energy. This is better for health, calms Self-preservation, and thrusts us towards prosperity.

Unfortunately, what is common for many of us is a personal energy shortage. This occurs when the way we manage our Self, our time, and the way we do things, uses up more energy than we produce. The rate of consumption is greater than our rate of regeneration. A personal energy shortage promotes poor health.

Here are some examples of personal energy shortage language and thoughts:
- I know what I don't want.
- I don't know what I want.
- I knew I should've done that.
- I went against my instinct even though I knew I would regret it.
- I'd love to do that but what will they think?

*The best thing that I've done
to maintain good Self-esteem,
is build a personal energy surplus.*

-- MICHAEL

- I never seem to have enough time.
  I feel tense and rushed.
- I have trouble sleeping. I wake up tired and feel angry.
- I often think negatively and beat my Self up.
- I feel fearful.
- I often over-react and feel out of control.
- I'm indecisive. I doubt my Self. I feel trapped.
- I get the negative "What ifs..."

Building Self-esteem is a wonderful process. Below are four suggestions to apply. Your Self-esteem will build and you will shift from a personal energy shortage to a personal energy surplus.

1. Remember the basics: food, water, and rest.
2. Focus on what you want to accomplish each day.
3. Become your own best friend and rooting section.
4. Take time for your Self.

The What ifs

THE WHAT IFS CAME TODAY
LEAVING ME SLUMPED IN A CHAIR,
HOLDING MY HEAD IN MY HANDS AND WONDERING,
AM I MAD?
AM I INSANE?
HAVE I LOST MY MIND?

I RAISE MY HEAD AND
CATCH A GLIMPSE OF MY SELF IN THE MIRROR
THE DEVASTATION ON MY FACE CONFIRMS MY WORST FEARS.
IT IS HOPELESS
RIDICULOUS
IT WILL NEVER WORK
PEOPLE WILL LAUGH
GIVE UP.

THE WHAT IFS HAD ME IN THEIR CLAWS
I WAS DEFEATED
I GAVE IN AND
LET THEM RULE MY MIND AND SOUL.

EVENTUALLY I STRUGGLE FROM THE CHAIR
SLOWLY THEY BEGIN TO LEAVE.
I WALK DOWN THE HALL WONDERING
WHAT PICTURE IN MY MIND'S EYE SENT THE INVITATION?
WHAT DID I SEE, HEAR,
OR FEEL THAT OPENED THE DOOR TO THE WHAT IFS?

I START TO SMILE AS THE PICTURE OF ALL MY DREAMS
COMING TRUE RETURNS
BUT I KNOW THEY'LL COME BACK,
THE WHAT IFS ALWAYS DO.
PERHAPS I'LL TAKE THEIR NAMES OFF THE GUEST LIST
AND HANG A SIGN IN MY MIND.
MR. & MRS. WHAT IF ARE NO LONGER INVITED.
THEY'VE WORN OUT THEIR WELCOME
ALL VISITATION RIGHTS ARE CANCELED.

THE WHAT IFS CAME TODAY...

--DINI PETTY

When our Self preservation reflex is in survival mode we loose the ability to tell the difference between a real threat and an imagined one. This is why a "What if" thought can cause such an unwanted reaction and create confusion. This can weaken our health and lower our Self-esteem. The way to solve this is to think first before we react. This is an important step in ending personal energy shortage.

List some situations
where you want to think before you react:

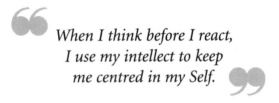

When I think before I react,
I use my intellect to keep
me centred in my Self.

-- SANDRA HARDING

Set up a rating system whereby you can judge how serious a situation really is. This will help you to learn from your Self to think before reacting. For example, spilling milk on the carpet might be a 1 out of 10. A child cutting his or her hand might be a 5 or 6. A serious health problem could be a 9. Rating situations is a good way to put the experience into perspective. How would you rate some situations of your own? Please fill in the box below.

> *When I'm playing soccer*
> *and I'm listening to my instinct*
> *I always know where the ball*
> *is going to be.*
> *My instinct tells me where*
> *I should be so that I am*
> *in a position to intercept the ball*
> *and sometimes score a goal.*

-- SHAUN

By having instinct lead and intellect follow, we can turn our personal energy shortage into a personal energy surplus. This is done by making sure we look after the basics, by considering where our instinct leads us, and by valuing our achievements. Good health is dependent on maintaining a consistent energy level and high Self-esteem thoughts.

Write down some high Self-esteem thoughts.

> *The key to tolerance*
> *is putting my needs first.*

--SANDRA

Instinct and Self-Esteem

LESSON 2: RELATIONSHIPS

In relationships, our primary relationship is with our Self. When we fulfill our obligation to our own needs we are more tolerant of others. When we ignore our needs we set our Self up for the following relationship scenario.

After working all day, Rachel gets home to be greeted by her daughter who wants help with her homework. At the same time her son is demanding dinner, and Frank, her partner, is flaked out on the couch. As the requests come pouring in, Rachel finds her Self flying into a rage and screaming, "No one cares for me! You expect me to do everything!"

Reacting happens when low Self-esteem permits us to ignore our own needs. We end up resenting others when they ask us to do things for them. When we have a personal energy shortage, we have a short fuse.

Here is a version of the above scenario with Rachel putting her needs first and coming from high Self-esteem.

Rachel has informed everyone that she needs a few minutes to get settled when she gets home. After working all day Rachel gets home, makes her Self a cup of tea, and sits down with her partner and daughter. She tells Frank where she would like help with dinner and explains to Rachel that she will help with her homework once they have eaten and cleaned up.

I used to be preoccupied with whether people would like me, particularly in new situations. Now I focus on the qualities that I like to see in a person and follow my instinct in choosing who I want to get to know. Learning to trust my instinct is helping me to rebuild my Self-esteem as I learn to value my Self and my opinions.

-- RENÉE

When we say "no one cares for us" what we are really saying is I have neglected to care for me. It's easier to work with instinct and take responsibility for fulfilling our basic needs. The result is a healthy balance between giving and taking. Positive emotions give us the personal energy to be happily involved with those around us and good Self-esteem lets us assert our wants and needs.

List the emotions you'd like to experience.
(For example: happy, loved, joyful, appreciated, sexy, fulfilled.)

"I used to consider my Self to be very amiable.
Now I realize that I was very agreeable
because I didn't value my opinions.
I let the opinions of others dominate mine
and I felt insecure and worthless.
When I started hearing and following my instinct,
I began to praise my Self for my thoughts.
I would communicate them, act on them,
and celebrate the effect of them.
I now like how I think about my Self.
I now have high Self-esteem.

-- KATHY

Learning To Mind our Own Business

In order to have the kind of relationships we want, it is necessary to stop being concerned with what others are thinking. We call this, learning to mind our own business. It's exhausting to worry about what others are thinking about us and could do to us.

Being overly concerned keeps us in our original relationship pattern, the one we shared with our parents. As a child, the only priority was to receive love and attention from others. Interaction was based on thoughts like, "What are they thinking?", or, "What can I do to make them notice me?" What can happen is our relationships all turn out being like the one we had with our parents.

This takes away from intimacy and from companionship. Divorce rates are high and people wonder why. To help turn this old pattern around, start caring about what we think of our Self first and stop caring about others thoughts and opinions.

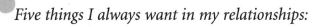*Five things I always want in my relationships:*

- *Treat my Self like I am good enough.*
- *Enjoy my mate.*
- *See my Self and my children healthy, happy, and Self-Directed.*
- *Attract ethical friends who add joy to my life.*
- *Truly enjoy my coworkers and what I do.*

-- DINI PETTY

Below, write some things you need to do for an instinctual relationship with your Self each day.

Lynda
- I learn everyday how to improve my communication skills. I am more aware of what I want and need in my life to maintain high Self-esteem.

Instinct and Self-Esteem

LESSON 3: LEARNING

In order to learn, we have to coordinate our thinking mind with our body reflex mind. Instinct is the part of us that is responsible for this. The coordination of these two parts in language is the phrase, *"I can do it!"* "I can" represents the mental part and "do it" represents the physical part. We learn from our Self how we can do it. A good example is how we learn the skills to be a good mother, father, child, student, wife, husband, or any role model. It may seem difficult at first, but as we gain experience over time we learn that we can do it.

Figure 2 is a chart describing the coordination of the thinking mind and the body reflex mind. When instinct is leading, we are in touch with our heart's desire and our choices for action are clearer and more concise. This sets up the "I can". The thinking mind sends the desired outcome message to the body reflex mind. The body reflex mind takes action and forms the "do it".

Achieving goals builds up the way we think about our Self, and raises Self-esteem. High Self-esteem and good feelings are the reward we get to encourage us to move forward. This makes the experience of learning a pleasure.

> *I love the feeling that comes from an 'I can do it' relationship with my Self*

--MICHEAL

FIGURE 2:

COORDINATING THE TWO MINDS

BUILDS SELF-CONFIDENCE AND
RAISES SELF-ESTEEM OVER TIME

MENTAL		PHYSICAL
THINKING MIND	INTEGRATES	BODY REFLEX MIND
'I CAN'		'DO IT'

INSTINCT COORDINATES

WHEN INSTINCT LEADS AND INTELLECT FOLLOWS,
WE SET UP AN "I CAN DO IT" RELATIONSHIP WITH OUR SELF.
WE ARE IN THE FRAME OF MIND TO LEARN.

> *When I speak in statements,*
> *I see children respond really well.*
> *I call this "playing my hand first."*

--SANDRA HARDING

Instinct and Self-Esteem

LESSON 4: LANGUAGE

To make a language of high Self-esteem we have to decide to treat our Self kindly and choose to respect our Self and others. Language, structure and Self-esteem are directly connected.

Low Self-esteem structure is to communicate in questions. The reason we communicate in questions is we are unsure of our Self and trying to control the other persons response. It is a defensive style. We hold back our true intent with one foot in and one foot out.

People, especially children have difficulty responding to questioning and get defensive. High Self-esteem structure is to communicate in statements. When communicating in statements we are sure of our Self and focused on presenting our point of view. It is a straight forward style. We put our true intent on the table - two feet in.

It is important to be aware of the language we use inside with our Self and say to others. If we notice negative language inside and we are speaking in questions, too much, it is important to stop and think about what it is we want to say. Once we are sure of our position we can speak in statements.

For example - "Did you clean up your room?" or "I think your room is still messy."

I used to get flustered at work
when I had a lot of deadlines.
Now I trust my instinct to organize my day
and get things done when I need to!

-- RENÉE

Instinct and Self-Esteem

LESSON 5: TIME MANAGEMENT

To get the most out of our time and to use our talents to the fullest, we need to be in performance mode. To be in performance mode, we must first make sure we are fully nourished. It is like putting gas in the car or charging up the cell phone batteries. Once nourished, it is effective to set goals and to focus on the outcome we want. This enables us to instinctually direct our energy and work towards our goals. Working this way boosts our energy. This makes a quiet mind and we enjoy what we do while maintaining focus from start to finish.

Self-esteem is raised when we become Self-confident and appreciate who we are and our ability to take care of our Self. Self-confidence is developed by becoming comfortable with our ability to do something. Reflecting on all the small things we do throughout one day, including eating, drinking water, and resting, adds up to a nourishing day. We are encouraging maximum performance and using time effectively.

*66 In golf, it is imperative to stay
in the 'present' for ideal performance.
I have learned, through Self-Directed Learning,
to trust my instincts, focus Inside/Out
and enjoy each moment that comes along!
I think the program is fabulous
because it has helped me to remain calm
and quiet in my mind
while I play my best golf!* 99

--NANCY

Make a list of accomplishments.

Self-Directed fashion; now that's style!

-- BRIAN

The Role of Intellect and Conscience

The focus of this book is getting to know and use instinct as the leader in Self-Direction. Part of understanding how to use instinct is learning to interpret our impulses to do things. It is the job of our intellect to check and make sure that we carry out our instinctual impulses. These are the impulses that make sense and produce actions that build up our health and are in line with our goals *(see Figure 3)*.

But when we have low Self-esteem our intellect gets in the way. At times we all have thoughts that go against our principles or our goals. This is sometimes referred to as sabotaging our Self. When we have these kinds of thoughts it is our instinct that kicks in and warns us to stop, think it through, and choose another option.

Instinct communicates with impulses in our body. Intellect is our logic response. When the two align we get a balanced feeling inside. This is a signal to proceed. When the two disagree we feel uncomfortable and this signals us to stop and think it through. Whenever we act without this agreement, we end up with a guilty feeling and this gets deposited in our conscience.

Conscience is a valuable thing. It helps keep us on track. This is why it is good to have a clear conscience. It shows we are using our intellect to interpret our instinct correctly to achieve our goals.

A good example of instinct and intellect working as a team is eating. When we get a hunger impulse (from our instinct), our intellect can go with it or not. We can either get something to eat or we can suppress that urge and eat later. In this case the goal is to find a balance so that we fulfill our nourishment needs.

INSTINCT AND INTELLECT COORDINATION

**FOLLOW THROUGH AND
MOVE TOWARDS GOAL**

**PUT ASIDE AND
THINK IT THROUGH**

INTELLECT CAN GO WITH IT OR AGAINST IT

IMPULSE TO DO SOMETHING

INSTINCT
(SELF)

WHEN INSTINCT AND INTELLECT DIFFER, REASSESS THE SITUATION.
THINK IT THROUGH MORE AND/OR SEEK ADVICE.
WHEN INSTINCT AND INTELLECT MATCH, WE CAN FOLLOW
THROUGH AND FOCUS ON OUR GOAL.

Intellect is the part of us that decides to go with or against our instinct. **Our instinct is always right.** Whenever we have a thought to do something a little crazy, it is up to us to use our intellect to reason it through and create the limits to ensure our safety and success. Then we are acting in our best interests.

Sorting the relationship between instinct and intellect is an ongoing process. The most energy efficient way for the two to work together is as good friends.

Instinct leads, intellect checks and then follows. When the two are in this relationship we are in prosperity mode. The result is a quiet mind and balanced feelings.

When the two are in an adversarial relationship we are in survival mode. At this point we argue with our Self and feel conflict.

The easiest way to train the two to work together as friends is to do the basics for our Self each day. Then it spills over into other aspects of our life and results in more harmony and confidence in our actions.

One of the best things parents can do to build up a child's Self-esteem is to show and communicate a constructive relationship between instinct and intellect. In this way we teach tomorrow's adults to act on impulses and thoughts that are good for their health.

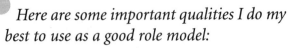 *Here are some important qualities I do my best to use as a good role model:*

- *Value doing the basics*
- *Hear and follow my instinct*
- *Think before taking action*
- *Communicate my thoughts constructively and listen to what I attract hearing from others*
- *Learn from my mistakes*
- *Celebrate my successes*

--Michael

Self-Directed Profiles

Where has learning to hear and follow your instinct affected your Self-esteem?

Pam   - My Self-esteem is at its highest peak ever in my life.

Kathy   - Learning to hear and follow my instinct has allowed me to rediscover my Self-esteem. I continue to build my Self-esteem because now I like my Self. With great respect and admiration for my Self, I have become my own best friend. I value how I feel, how I think, what I say, and what I do. I covet and will forever nurture this friendship I have with my Self.

Michelle   - After a while, a Self-love for who you are and what you are capable of achieving comes into play. It is kind of like being a peacock and then realizing that you have all these feathers to show off!

Gitte   - Now that I hear and follow my instinct, I feel that I am beautiful through and through. My thoughts are pleasing to me, I spend much more time letting my mind wander and discover the intricacies of life--to live. To be part of the great universe. To be part of a greater life. I deserve it. I love to feel special and love to say that I am special. I impart my thoughts to others and feel special because my instinct comes first and I hear it loud and clear. I follow my instinct.

Lynda   - I have found my Self moving forward in my respect for my decisions and my feelings of Self-worth and it is easier to admit and forgive my Self for my mistakes.

*I want to believe every student
will leave high school with a healthy,
fully functioning connection
to instinct and high Self-esteem.*

-- DINI PETTY

Self-esteem

Main ingredient:

Increased Self-confidence naturally creates a language of Self-value. This builds Self-esteem and adds to a personal energy surplus.

Write to Make Right

_____

_____

_____

_____

_____

_____

_____

_____

_____

_____

_____

_____

_____

_____

"When I write about something,
I can make it right for me." -- SANDRA HARDING

-138-

_____

_____

_____

_____

_____

_____

_____

_____

_____

_____

_____

_____

_____

_____

_____

_____

_____

_____

_____

Instinct AND Processing In/Out

$\mathcal{T}$HE FOURTH STAGE IN THE DEVELOPMENT
OF THE BUTTERFLY IS BIRTH. THIS IS WHERE
THE BUTTERFLY LEAVES THE CHRYSALIS TO EMBARK
ON ITS SELF-DIRECTED JOURNEY AS A BUTTERFLY.

I'm inside looking out.
Why would I think Outside/In.

-- MATTHEW

There is Processing In/Out and there is Out/In processing. We will describe Out/In processing first because this has been the way we have learned most things.

Out/In processing is defined as a way of taking in information that considers the opinions, desires, and viewpoints of others before our own. We learned to educate our intellect this way. However, this goes against our instinct. It makes our minds over-active and drains our body of energy. The name Out/In processing means that we interpret situations from outside of our Self in the surrounding environment and then move that information inside our Self. When we process this way, it empowers the opinions of others to decide how we feel about our Self.

Out/In processing uses questioning language to control how others respond. For example, Jesse thinks of telling her mate something, so she structures her language in an attempt to keep him from over-reacting. Her focus is on what he might think, say, or do, instead of what she wants to say.

Our language to our Self and to others is very important. Out/In processing language is emotionally led and our feelings of safety and Self-esteem are based on the responses and actions of other people. Here are examples of Out/In energy draining language:

- "Do I look O.K.?"
- "Does he think I'm attractive?"
- "Even when I'm alone, I am trying to please them."
- "Everybody is looking at me."
- "I wonder what they'll think of my makeup?"
- "Will they think I look fat?"
- "I hope this doesn't upset them."

Renée - *I used to focus on my outside appearance when it came to defining my beauty. I compared my Self to images in the media and to other people who I thought were in better shape or more beautiful than I was. I chastised my Self for not looking the same. However, over time I began to realize that my beauty is my own and it radiates from who I am rather than from what I look like. I look at my Self now and see a beautiful woman both on the inside and outside.*

The remedy for Out/In processing is Processing In/Out. This is taking care of our Self first and creates the desired good feelings of high Self-esteem and energy. Building up our own energy level comes from fulfilling our Self-preservation needs first. We put the needs of others after satisfying our own. Now, let's look at some examples of In/Out energy building language:

- "I look good."
- "That person looks interesting, I would like to introduce my Self."
- "I like that woman across the room. I'd like to meet her."
- "I'm looking at you looking at me. I'm checking you out."
- "This is the best hair style I've ever had. It is definitely a good hair day."
- "I feel comfortable in these clothes."
- "I can do it."
- "I want to buy something for my Self today."

When we Process In/Out we consider our opinion before theirs. It is the opposite direction than Out/In processing as it moves information from our Self outwards. Processing In/Out works with instinct, makes the mind calm, and charges up the body. We can decide how things affect us when we process this way.

> *When I'm centred in my Self,*
> *I take the time to think*
> *about my feelings, this keeps me*
> *Processing In/Out.*

-- SANDRA HARDING

In your own words, describe the difference
between processing information In/Out and Out/In.

Pam - My health is excellent. Whenever I start to feel run down or feel a cold or flu coming, I listen to my instinct and take time out for me. The colds stay away.

Instinct and Processing In/Out

LESSON 1: HEALTH

Taking responsibility for our personal health management is an essential skill to develop. Since birth, most of us learned to believe that others know more about our well being than we do. From mothers and fathers, to teachers and doctors, we have come to depend on others to make choices for us that we really need to make for our Self. When we allow others to tell us what is best for us and follow their advice without checking it with our intellect and instinct, this exemplifies Out/In processing.

It is the job of our instinct to keep us in good health. As a result of Out/In processing, the part of our instinct responsible for taking care of our health is under-developed. It is difficult to feel confident about the choices we make for our personal healthcare when we are out of touch with our instinct.

It is important to have trained specialists in healthcare. However, it is just as important to take responsibility in the decision-making process and choose what is right for us. It is wrong to place this responsibility upon our healthcare professionals.

Caring for our own health and knowing what is best for our Self is instinctive. The idea is to collect information and opinions from the healthcare system to help us make informed choices for our Self. Our instinct always knows what is best. Accepting responsibility for our own health enables us to be our own authority as we naturally Process In/Out.

66 *When I Process In/Out,*
I'm in touch with my instinct .
Asthma attacks are
a thing in my past, since I learned how
to manage my health. *99*

-- MICHAEL

Self-preservation instinct and health are directly related. As we develop a connection to our instinct we gain confidence interacting with the healthcare system from an In/Out point of view. The more Self-confidence we have the better we use our problem solving abilities. This naturally raises our Self-esteem and we anticipate success.

Of all the lessons, the one about food, water, and rest has been one of the most difficult for me. It sounds simple. Why did I have trouble with it? It's because I learned that the needs of others were more important than mine. Now I take time for eating, I rest when I'm tired, and I drink water when my body is thirsty. Giving these things to my Self has become a pleasure.

-- DINI PETTY

List some occasions when you have followed
the advice of others when you wanted to follow your own:

> *I spent years being everyone's court jester,*
> *always concerned with everyone liking me*
> *and putting their feelings before mine.*
> *I saw a dramatic change after thirty two years of*
> *Out/In processing while having coworkers over one*
> *night, only eight months after beginning my own*
> *Self-Directed Journey. My partner mentioned that*
> *everyone in the living room was just staring at each*
> *other and I had better get in there and do something.*
> *It was the first time I can recall my instinct having*
> *an unobstructed path to my lips and I quickly said,*
> *'Why would I want to go in there?'*
> *My fun was more important to me than*
> *my guests momentary lapse in conversation.*
> *My usual guilt was gone...*
> *this was a big step for me!*

-- JEFF

Review these situations. Based on what you have just
learned, rewrite the same scenerios following instinct.

Kathy - *Learning to hear and follow my instinct has greatly affected my relationships because now I respect my Self and I hear others respecting me too. I like how I feel with people I choose to spend time with. In/Out rules!*

Instinct and Processing In/Out

LESSON 2: RELATIONSHIPS

We have learned an Out/In system of serving others before our Self. In our relationships this is considered normal. Putting our Self first is often interpreted as being selfish. However, putting others first is a direct threat to our Self-preservation as it is designed to take care of our own needs first. When we take care of our Self first, we are better able and more willing to take care of others. When we serve others first, our responses are resentful and our feelings are negative because we are going against our instinct. This builds on itself especially when we feel that the other party doesn't give back equally.

Processing In/Out in relationships means that we consider our needs first to maintain a good relationship with our Self. Then we can do things for another. This is the best way to honour the Self-preservation part of our instinct. When we follow this order we are nourished by giving. This is giving from a full heart.

In a marriage or relationship the In/Out priority order is Self, mate, children, family, friends, coworkers, and business relations.

*There have been many times in my life
when I would agree to do something
or go somewhere only to realize after the fact
that I didn't really want to. I was more concerned
about pleasing others or doing what I thought
others expected of me. As I am learning to hear
and follow my instinct before deciding
my course of action, I now find my Self
in these situations less and less.*

-- RENÉE

List some situations where you have put the needs of other people before your own and it still bothers you.

I treat my husband and children
with the same respect I give to my
business associates

-- SANDRA HARDING

What did you think when you put their needs before yours?

*I know when I'm putting
their needs before mine,
because I'm unhappy.*

--SANDRA

Rewrite these situations putting your needs first.

Pam - *I learn at my own pace and stay focused on my activity of the moment. There is a purpose to everything that I do.*

Instinct and Processing In/Out

LESSON 3: LEARNING

There are two Me's: 'Inside Me' and 'Outside Me'. 'Inside Me' is connected to our Self and expresses our true nature. It is where we feel our instinct. 'Inside Me' always Processes In/Out and considers our Self and our opinions first, and then others.

'Outside Me' is a learned behaviour in our intellect developed as a coping skill to please others. Here is an Out/In processing scenario:

Friends are going out to eat at a place that I don't like. I would rather go out with my wife to a movie. Yet I allow my Self to be talked into going and pretend to have a good time even though I spend the whole evening wishing I wasn't there. This learned behaviour in 'Outside Me' switches on to pretend I am having a good time, when I really wish I was somewhere else. It's how I learned to act around others. Everyone would have been better off if I let 'Inside Me' lead and did what I wanted to.

As this example shows, 'Outside Me' processes Out/In and ignores our own instinct by doing what we think will please the other person, so we don't hurt their feelings. This is what we learned when we were young, but now we must get the two Me's working together as soon as possible.

An adult version of the two Me's is 'Inside Me' -- the boss, and 'Outside Me' -- the worker. 'Outside Me' carries out and follows through on 'Inside Me's' decisions and directions. This returns us to our instinctive way of processing information which was buried out of necessity when we were children.

Gitte

- *My instinct is healthy, strong, and beautiful. Therefore, I am healthy, strong, and beautiful. The process is simple: In-Out. The feelings inside must come outside in the form of speech or writing to strengthen my immune system to heal, to make me beautiful and strong. It is all encompassing in two short words, IN - OUT.*

A common experience for many of us, is the battle between 'Inside Me' and 'Outside Me'. We learned to interpret things as black and white. We learned that there are opposing forces in almost everything. As a result, when we try to decide in our mind about something, we cannot. We have as many reasons not to do something as we have to do it. Internal and external arguing becomes a way of life. A lot of inner conflict is eliminated when we re-educate our intellect that 'Inside Me' directs 'Outside Me' that they learn to work together like two sides of the same coin. After all, that is what they are. The result is less inner argument.

Draw a picture of your two "Me's" working together.

Michelle - *My language is more positive. I have learned to say I want, I can, and I will instead of I don't! I won't! I can't!.*

Please read each of the statements below and write
a description of you experiencing them.

1. *I am comfortable with my Self.*

2. *I act instinctively.*

3. *I foresee what I want.*

4. *I use "I can do it" language.*

> *In/Out is where it's more important to be happy than to be right.*

--SANDRA HARDING

Instinct and Processing In/Out

LESSON 4: LANGUAGE

Here is a technique we call making your own middle ground. It uses language to coordinate 'Inside Me' and 'Outside Me' to work together constructively. Doing this helps us to hear our instinct and use our thoughts better as we discover more on our Self-Directed Journey.

(A) **INSIDE ME**	(B) **JOINING WORD**	(C) **OUTSIDE ME**
Thinks		Reacts
Chooses		Carries out choice
Starts things		Finishes things

Under (B), write three words joining Inside me to Outside me. (For example, Thinks - **Pauses** - Reacts, Chooses - **Prepares** - Carries out choice, Starts things - **Loves** - Finishes things.) Please use coloured pencils or crayons for this exercise.

> *Getting my young son to bed used to be*
> *a real challenge. I would tell him he had to go*
> *to bed early so that he wouldn't be tired or miserable*
> *in the morning. We would argue and inevitably*
> *I would see him waking up tired*
> *and miserable most mornings.*
>
> *When I began processing my thoughts*
> *and language In/Out, I put my Self first*
> *in my communications with my son.*
> *Now at bedtime, I tell him that I want to have*
> *quiet time for my Self so that I can take a bath,*
> *read a book, or watch television.*
>
> *I consider my wants and needs first.*
> *I communicate my feelings with honesty*
> *and respect to my Self. Bedtime is now*
> *a pleasant end to my day and*
> *my son's day as well.*

--KATHY

After you have chosen your words, think about coordinating your 'Inside Me' and your 'Outside Me'. Take your coloured pencils or crayons and choose any colour which you feel drawn to. Using this colour, either circle your middle words or shade the area where your words are written to integrate them.

Next, read the joining words in column B from the top of the list to the bottom. As soon as you finish, write down the first letter that comes to mind in the space provided here.

1. LETTER

Next, read the joining words in column B from the bottom word to the top. Again, write down the first letter that comes to mind in the space provided.

2. LETTER

Now, using the letters you have chosen, think of a word for each of them and fill them in the spaces provided below.

3. WORD	4. WORD

"WOW! I feel like a kid again!
For years, I battled my inner demons Self-doubt.
I have learned through Self-Direction
to be my own best friend.
Golf is fun again
and I'm enjoying the journey!

--CHRIS

Now, read your last two words together and pick a final letter. Make that letter into a word that describes you using
your instinct in the box below. This is
your trigger word. By using this trigger
word, you keep your instinct in charge,
so that 'Inside Me' is leading and
'Outside Me' is following. This is
Processing In/Out.

LETTER

WORD

Finally, write/draw your trigger word/picture in your
chosen colour in the large box entitled "Personal Symbol
for Instinct" on the next page. You can use this like a cue
card for your instinct at any time to keep your mind
focused. For example, if you are feeling conflict about a
situation, imagine your personal symbol. Breathe deeply.
Exhale with a sigh. This helps to restore your inner
balance and Self-Direction.

*My mental chatter has quieted
since my two Me's
work together.*

--MICHAEL

MY PERSONAL SYMBOL FOR INSTINCT

My instinct is me.
My intellect knows me.

--MATTHEW

Before moving on to the next lesson here is a review of the steps and techniques we have explained to help you in your Self-Directed Journey.

- The Basics: Food, Water, and Rest.

- Hear and follow your instinct.

- Think before taking action.

- Use "I can do it" language.

- Use "what I want" foresight

- Process In/Out

- The Muscle Memory Release Technique.

- Mental Trash Elimination writing Technique.

- Using your Personal Symbol for Instinct

- Focus on what you accomplish

- Speak in statements

- Focus in the present

- Use "Kind to Self" language

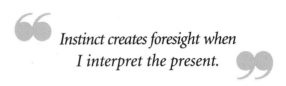

*Instinct creates foresight when
I interpret the present.*

--SANDRA HARDING

Write out a daily routine for your Self
choosing from the list on previous page.

Kathy - *Learning to hear and follow my instinct has taught me to manage my time more effectively. Putting my needs and wants first, I organize and prioritize my time to allow my Self to remain in the present and do what is best for me.*

Instinct and Processing In/Out

LESSON 5: TIME MANAGEMENT

When we follow instinct in our time management we are empowered by our Self to organize our day from an In/Out perspective. In/Out means we consider what we want to do with our time so that we accomplish what we want each day. This builds motivation and satisfaction.

Out/In time management means we consider what others want us to do with our time. If we have enough time left over at the end of the day, we can do something we want to do. Out/In time management goes against instinct, makes struggle, and contributes to burn out. As a result, there is a constant tension accompanied with a sense of being short of time.

In order to prevent this, it is important to direct our time management from an In/Out perspective each day.

We suggest taking a few minutes each morning to write a list of things you want to get done.

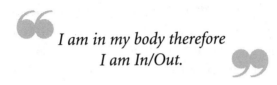

I am in my body therefore
I am In/Out.

-- Sandra Harding

Self-Directed Profiles

What does Processing In/Out mean to you?

Pam - I receive and organize information as I want to rather than as how I think someone would like. I create and manage my own environment - rather than it rule me.

Kathy - Processing In/Out means putting my Self first in my thoughts. When I hear and listen to my Self I automatically put my Self first. I think about how I feel and what I want. I respect my process with integrity and honesty to my Self. I say and do what is best for me.

Michelle - I think and look for the answer within my Self before turning to others for your answers. Think first, find your solution, and then react.

Gitte - To Process In/Out is to put into thoughts what my instinct is feeling. Cause and effect. First comes the feeling inside my chest. It immediately translates into an image that turns into thoughts that are communicated to the outside world.

Lynda - It means that I make my choices and follow through in my actions, after processing my thoughts and instinctual feelings inside to the outside world around me.

Self-Direction is heart directed.
It is my divine heritage and birthright.
It is me whole and holy coming from my
instinctual core which is my centre of purity.
It is me creating a life for my Self that is truly happy,
peaceful, and prosperous, just the way
I've always dreamt it could be.
Being able to hear my heart, trust it,
and act on it is the gift of heaven on earth.
It is the best gift ever.

Once I was a shattered soul, broken into what seemed
to be a million pieces. My inner dialogue was a
boggled mess of short circuits;
my life experience was one of suffering,
loss and despair. In these last five years, I have been
learning how to hear my heart's voice and trust my
ever-wise instinct. That reality of sadness has
become history for me.
For the most part, now I am happy in every moment
and I feel safe where I am. At long last,
the love in my heart is welcomed and honoured
by those who receive it.

My life grows richer and more fulfilling as each month
unfolds. Importantly, I have come to know that no matter
what happens around me, I'm okay, I will be okay,
and I will make the choices that are for my
highest good. As a result, everyone else is
lovingly cared for as well. No more carrying another's
burden. This new way of living my life is a great
feeling and it gives me a great freedom to be who I am.
Yes, Self-Direction is heart directed.
It's the natural instinct.
I am joyful and thankful to be remembering
the beautiful voice of my most precious heart.

--Ross

Processing In/Out

<u>Main Ingredient:</u>

To focus on thinking about what we want to say rather than how the person is going to respond. This is an example of Processing In/Out and keeps our two me's working together.

Write to Make Right

_____

_____

_____

_____

_____

_____

_____

_____

_____

_____

_____

_____

_____

_____

"When I write about something,
    I can make it right for me."   -- SANDRA HARDING

Conclusion

*L*IVING LIFE AS A BUTTERFLY

FOLLOWING INSTINCT'S LEAD.

THE RECIPE FOR SELF-DIRECTION

I GET WHAT I WANT

**EXERCISE SELF-AUTHORITY
PROCESS IN/OUT**

CREATES A LANGUAGE OF HIGH SELF-ESTEEM

**BUILDS SELF-CONFIDENCE.
DECIDE TO RESPECT
MY SELF AND OTHERS**

**OPENS A CHANNEL TO INSTINCT AND USES
INTELLECT TO GO WITH INSTINCT TO DO THINGS**

**DOING THE BASICS:
FOOD, WATER, REST**

START HERE

USE TECHNIQUES TO MAINTAIN
AN OPEN CHANNEL TO YOUR INSTINCT

Our journey has brought us through the four stages of the conception, development, and birth of the butterfly. It is a Self-Directed Journey. A journey to Self-realization.

Figure 4 illustrates the steps involved in the recipe for Self-Direction. Please start from the bottom of the chart and move upwards.

The first step is to do the basics so our nourishment needs are met. This is the easiest way to put our Self first. Our instinct shifts us into prosperity mode. Then we use our intellect to choose things that are constructive to our overall goals.

By taking the time to nuture our Self and acting on constructive choices, we are respecting our Self. This opens the door to respecting others. We build Self-confidence as we get to know what is best from our Self and go with our instinct to accomplish our goals.

High Self-esteem is the natural result when we are confident in our ability to Self-Direct and respectfully express who we are to our Self and to others. "I can do it" language helps us think kindly of our Self and of others. We create good, balanced feelings inside.

Processing In/Out guarantees we stay inside our balanced feelings and exercise our Self-authority. This works with our natural instinct and tends to our over-reactive responses. As we get what we want, we believe in our Self and enjoy the harmony that occurs when instinct leads and intellect follows. Then we are the most beautiful we can be inside and out.

*I enjoy seeing, feeling and acting from my Self
and learning to ignore the tapes of how
I'm supposed to see, feel and act.
I am being true to my Self.*

-- RENÉE

We are all different and we are the only ones who can understand our own personal mission in life. Instinct, Self-confidence, Self-esteem, and Processing In/Out are the ingredients of true Self-Direction and this ensures we can get what we want.

Make a list of what you want. Start with your health first.

FIGURE 5:

MY SELF DIRECTS INSTINCTIVELY

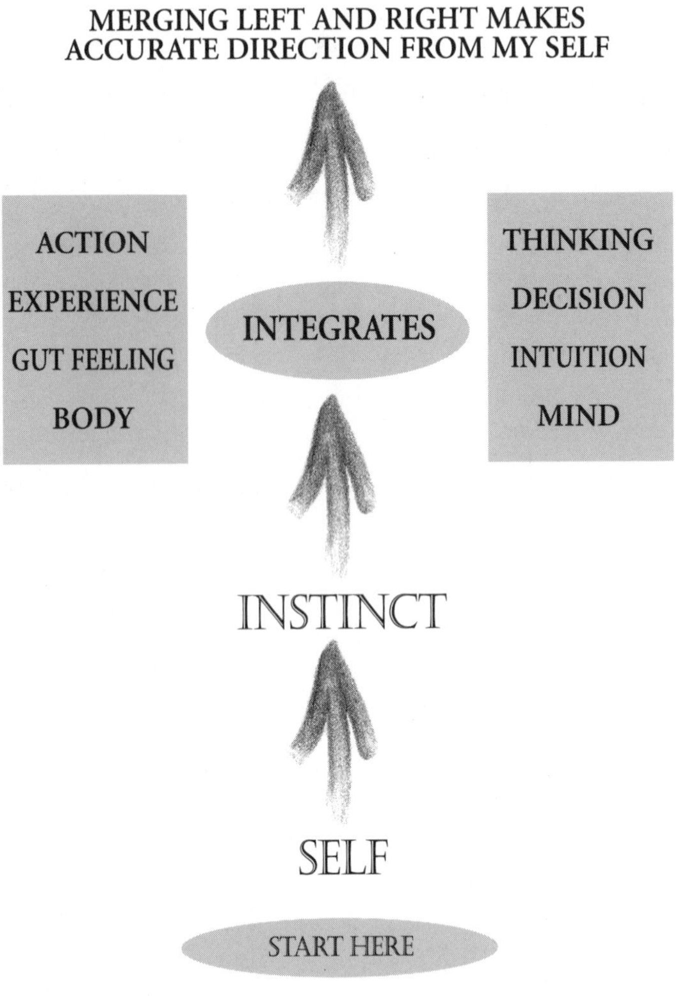

**MERGING LEFT AND RIGHT MAKES
ACCURATE DIRECTION FROM MY SELF**

ACTION		THINKING
EXPERIENCE	**INTEGRATES**	DECISION
GUT FEELING		INTUITION
BODY		MIND

INSTINCT

SELF

START HERE

INSTINCT IS THE PART OF US THAT CAN COORDINATE
ALL OF US (BODY AND MIND) IN ONE DIRECTION.

With the development of Self-authority comes the responsibility to use it to create win/win scenarios for everyone. By building our own Self-authority constructively and integrating it, we are also helping others to build theirs as well. This is the joy of sharing our wisdom and our Self with others. This is the gift that the butterfly represents, the transformation from survival living into a life of prosperity.

The bottom line is to get in touch with *your* instinct and learn to use it. This is Self-Direction and true understanding, freedom to know and to be your Self. It may be awkward at first, like learning to ride a bike or drive a car. Stay with it. Soon you'll get good at sensing what is best for you and knowing how to Self-Direct.

Figure 5 is a chart which shows how we Self-Direct instinctively to do what is best for us. It shows how our instinct coordinates the direction of our thoughts and actions. You will notice that we have positioned instinct at the bottom of the chart. This is because in Self-Directed Learning, instinct is the root. *Figure 5* shows the results of applying the information in A Self-Directed Journey.

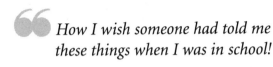 *How I wish someone had told me these things when I was in school!*

--DINI PETTY

CONTINUING TO USE THIS JOURNAL

We congratulate you on your completion of this journey. The more you review and use the information in this book, the better you will get at listening to and following instinct. Now that you are well on your Self-Directed Journey, you may continue to use this book in any way. One of our favourite ways to do this, is to ask our Self a question and open the book instinctively at any page to read the answer.

SHARING THE VISION

"What I want is to present
my recipe for Self-Direction.
My desire is to see others have
the opportunity to make a better life,
learning to be true to Self."

-- SANDRA HARDING

Many of the problems we see in today's society can be resolved with the development and use of Self-Directing skills. These are the tools that promote functional relationships, not only with our Self and in our families, but also within our society at large. These are the instinctive skills necessary for finding our creative potentials and following our dreams to fulfillment. The information contained in this book becomes a bridge we can all use to move from a mindset and lifestyle of struggle, fear, and survival to one of security, calm, and prosperity.

Glossary

Automatic Behaviours: Those behaviours which are learned and accessed by memory.

In/Out: A method of processing language, perceiving the world from inside the body looking out. eg. Focusing on what we want.

Instinct: The inate messenger of our Self. The part of us that knows what is best for us.

Intellect: The logic response to instinct's direction.

Muscle/Body Reflex: The body's physical response to situations.

Out/In Processing: A method of processing language, perceiving the world from the outside/in. eg. Focusing on what they are going to do.

Personal Energy Surplus: When we produce more energy than we consume.

Personal Energy Shortage: When we consume more energy than we produce.

Self-Preservation: The most primary sense responsible for survival first and prosperity second.

Self-Esteem: How I think about my Self inside.

Self-Confidence: My ability to hear and follow my instinct so I believe I can do it.

Self-Directing Skills: Skills to coordinate body and mind in the same direction.

Write to Make Right

_____

_____

_____

_____

_____

_____

_____

_____

_____

_____

_____

_____

_____

"When I write about something,
  I can make it right for me." -- SANDRA HARDING

_____

_____

_____

_____

_____

_____

_____

_____

_____

_____

_____

_____

_____

_____

_____

_____

_____

_____

_____

_____

_____

_____

_____

_____

_____

_____

_____

_____

_____

_____

_____

Instinct

Main ingredient:
Use the basics.
This is the best way to put your
self first, tuning into and developing
a relationship with your instinct.

Self-confidence

Main ingredient:
Prioritize having instinct lead your
decisions so it becomes familiar.
Believe in your Self-Direction
to build an attitude of confidence.

Self-esteem

Main ingredient:
Increased Self-confidence naturally
creates a language of Self-value.
This builds Self-esteem and adds
to a personal energy surplus.

Processing In/Out

Main Ingredient:
To focus on thinking about what we
want to say rather than how the
person is going to respond. This is an
example of Processing In/Out and keeps
our two me's working together.

ρ

$\mathcal{T}$o order **A Self-Directed Journey**
book and/or cassette
please fill in the information below.

☐ **A Self-Directed Journey - The Recipe**
Book
$19.95 + G.S.T. and shipping

☐ **A Self-Directed Journey - The Beginning**
Cassette Tape
$12.95 + G.S.T.+ P.S.T. and shipping

☐ **Order both for**
$29.95 + G.S.T.+ P.S.T. and shipping

The Self-Directed Learning Place
121 Old Forest Hill Road, Unit 1
Toronto, Ontario, M5N 2N6

PHONE: 1-800-303-5013
FAX: 416-256-0531
WEBSITE: www.selfdirect.com

CARDHOLDERS: ☐ VISA ☐ MASTERCARD

SIGNATURE_____

CARD#_____

EXPIRY DATE_____

. . . .

NAME: _____

ADDRESS: _____

CITY: _____ PROV. : _____

POSTAL CODE: _____

PHONE NUMBER: _____

✂
. . . .
DELIVERY WITHIN 4 WEEKS

A Self-Directed Journey - The Beginning

Cassette Tape of the speech, "Using Instinct" - Delivered by
Canadian Talk Show Host Dini Petty. Also featuring
Canadian Designer Brian Bailey and Recording Artist,
Billy Newton-Davis.

Coming next in the Self-Directed Journey Series:
Training the Intellect

Our Intellect can make the difference between success
and failure, motivation and apathy. In our next book we
provide key principles to maintaining emotional balance
and minimizing internal mental argument. We present a
four-part system consisting of the conscious, sub-conscious
and unconscious minds as well as our body reflex.

When the four parts are aligned we choose constructive
thoughts. When they are mixed up we generate destructive
thoughts which get in the way and sabotage us. Training the
intellect by using instinct maximizes our Self-Directing
abilities to focus and achieve what we set out to do. This
book shows how to train your intellect so you stop being
angry with your Self and become your own best friend.

INDIVIDUAL AND GROUP COURSES AVAILABLE.
CONTACT US FOR MORE INFORMATION:

The Self-Directed Learning Place
121 Old Forest Hill Road, Unit 1
Toronto, Ontario M5N 2N6
Phone: 1-800-303-5013
Fax: (416) 256-0531
WEBSITE: www.selfdirect.com

Sandra Harding lives in Toronto with her husband.
Together they run The Self-Directed Learning Place.

———◈———

Dini Petty and her partner live in a country home
north of Toronto. Her talk show on the CTV network
is in its tenth season and Dini divides her time
between television and various business projects.